Thank you for your passion
for reaching the lost

12/7/06 Allen

Lk 1-38

Gallon-Size Faith *in a* Pint-Size Book

Series

Forgiveness:

Where Real Life and Faith Come Together

Gallon-Size Faith in a Pint-Size Book

Series

Forgiveness:

Where Real Life and Faith Come Together

Dr. Allen R. Hunt

Signature Editions

Atlanta, Georgia

9820 Nesbit Ferry Road, Alpharetta, GA 30022
PHONE: 678-336-3000
http://www.allenhuntshow.com/
http://mountpisgah.org/

PUBLISHED BY SIGNATURE EDITIONS
4875 Markim Forest Lane, Sugar Hill, GA 30518
877-9PRINT5 www.signature-editions.net

Nouns and pronouns referring to deity are capitalized throughout the text of this book unless they are included within a direct quotation, in which case the original capitalization is retained.

Includes bibliographical references.

ISBN-10: 0-9776892-4-7
ISBN-13: 978-0-9776892-4-8

Printed in the United States of America
First Printing December 2006

DEDICATION

For Anita,

A Grace-Filled Forgiver

Acknowledgements

No book is possible without the contributions of many persons. Life and ministry are a team sport, and so is writing. I am deeply grateful to Hong Ke for her passion for excellence and hard work on details, to Jeanette Dickens for her regular prodding to pursue this venture, to Glenn Davenport for his support in making this idea a reality, and to the incredible people of Mount Pisgah. God is good.

Contents

Contents

INTRODUCTION

The toughest words in the English language are "I forgive you." Frankly, I'm not very good at forgiveness. Truth be told, my two teenage daughters have taught me more about forgiveness than I have ever taught them. It seems to come naturally to them. I apologize, they forgive, and forgive gladly, with no grudges.

Unfortunately, I have found that many adults—unlike my daughters—are not quite so fluent in forgiveness, even though forgiveness is at the center of our faith. This powerful emotion lies at the very heart of God.

I have written this little book to remind me just how powerful the force of forgiveness can be in my life. I hope it reminds you, too.

Forgiveness lies squarely at the intersection of real life and faith. When we are unable or unwilling to forgive, bitterness takes root in our souls and infects our everyday life. Bitterness pollutes every relationship. However, when we receive God's forgiveness, we can forgive others. When we forgive, we discover my favorite word in all the world: grace.

This book is about grace—the grace of God and the amazing power of forgiveness in the lives of people. Some stories are small and some are large; some ordinary, a few bordering on the miraculous. All of them are remarkable stories of the marvelous things God does when we share His grace with one another as generously as He has given it to us.

This book is about grace—the grace of God and the amazing power of forgiveness in the lives of people.

1

Forgiveness Sets You Free

Forgiveness is never small, ever sweet,
and it always sets you free.

Several years ago, shortly after becoming a pastor at my church, I experienced a church clash of such grand proportions that it became the worst conflict to date in my life and ministry. It started with a disagreement between the church and the board of directors of the grade school affiliated with the church. Board members, school parents, church members, friends, colleagues—everyone chose sides. The tumult was bitter, ugly, and hostile. As the new pastor on the staff, I brought a fresh perspective and a measure of objectivity. I became chief public spokesman and principal worker seeking resolution to this divisive situation.

This placed me before large groups of people in public meetings, often with dozens, sometimes even hundreds of people attending—sometimes members or leaders, other times school parents, or the school board of directors. None of these meetings were fun.

One group was the most painful—the parents. At several parents' meetings I encountered a mother who had two children enrolled in the school.

She was not only angry and bitter, she was also vocal, and she never seemed to have a kind word to say to anyone. She did not trust me at all—not in the least. She questioned everything I said and always responded harshly. This conflict dragged on at meeting after meeting for more than a year. It literally wore me out, and I still bear the scars from the battles.

This mother's children remained enrolled in the school for one year after the conflict began. That year became the longest of my life, not only because of her but also because of the tension throughout the entire school each day. I did my best to avoid her and move on with my life and my new ministry at the church, but instead of dealing with the feelings inside of me, I repressed them. I found it increasingly hard to trust other people.

Unforgiveness took root in my heart, and bitterness crept into my emotions and my relationships.

One year after the conflict, this mother and her children moved to another school. I felt relieved that I would no longer have to encounter her or see the anger and bitterness in her eyes, but I could still feel the resentment in my heart.

Later that year, our school and her children's new school played a tennis match. I decided to stop by the courts and watch for a few minutes on the way home, not thinking that this mother would be there. My heart sank when I saw her walking up to me. My stomach clenched. I braced myself for what was coming.

However, instead of the venom I was expecting, she said something like, "Allen, I want to apologize to you. These last few years have been very hard, and I realize now that you were telling me the truth. I was very ugly to you, and I apologize. I'm sorry. Please forgive me." She took the first step.

To be honest, I have never been more surprised in my life. To be even more honest, I have never felt that free in my life. It was the most genuine apology I have ever received in my life from anyone, much less a woman I barely knew who had verbally assaulted me. I should have prayed for her, but I was unable to do so because of my own sinfulness and unwillingness to deal with the hurt I felt. When I hurt someone in the future, I can only hope that I will be able to show that kind of spiritual honesty. I know that experience was a struggle for me so that I could learn something about myself. She has taught me much.

She took the first step, the step I should have taken. She showed me grace when I could not do the same for her.

REAL LIFE HELPS

A couple who had been married for 15 years began having more than their share of disagreements. They wanted to make their marriage work and agreed on an idea for change. Once a day, for one month, they agreed that each of them would write down something they didn't like about the other and drop the slip of paper in a "Fault Box." The boxes would provide a less confrontational way to let each spouse know about their daily irritations. The wife was diligent in her efforts to fill the Fault Box with issues she had with her husband each and every day: "Leaving the jelly top off the jar." "Wet towels on the shower floor." "Dirty socks not in hamper." The comments went on and on until the end of the month when one evening after dinner they exchanged boxes. The husband opened his box and reflected on all the reminders of what he had done wrong. Then the wife opened her box and began reading. The

Learn to forgive in the small things. The large ones will soon follow. Jesus said, "Forgive us our debts, as we also have forgiven our debtors" (Matthew 6:12)

slips of paper were all the same. The message on each slip of paper read simply, "I love you!"

SEVEN STEPS TO FORGIVENESS

Seven steps you can take toward a lifestyle of forgiveness

1. First, remember your own need for forgiveness. Admit that you are imperfect, yet God still loves you immeasurably. You are forgiven; therefore, you can forgive.

2. Clearly define only one thing that someone has done to you that you know you ought to forgive. Don't try to forgive it all at once.

3. Pray and ask God to saturate you with a spirit of grace. You cannot forgive on your own. The task is too large. With God's help, the task becomes small.

4. Engage the "offender" in direct, open, and honest communication. Be compassionate even in confrontation.

5. Follow up with some act of reconciliation—perhaps an outing together, a "kiss and make up" exchange, a hug or a handshake.

6. To prevent the same hurts from occurring again, keep your lines of communication open, with clear boundaries and guidelines for your relationship.

7. Learn to forgive the small things—with friends, family members, spouse. Don't dwell on the small hurts that we all experience daily and, frankly, that we all cause in others. Give the grace you wish to receive. Learn to say, "I love you."

PRAYER: *Forgiving God, I want to have a heart like Yours. Guide my steps today so that I will not fall into the trap of harboring unforgiveness in small things. Those little grudges add up. Teach me to love as You love.*

2

FORGIVENESS TAKES COURAGE

Forgiveness is not optional, and requires spiritual strength.

During the Nazi occupation of Holland during World War II, Casper ten Boom ran a watchmaker's shop in the lower floor of his home in the Dutch city of Haarlem. Upstairs, his daughter Corrie was the chief organizer of an underground movement to rescue the Jews. Until their arrest in February 1944, the ten Booms helped approximately 800 Jews to escape.

Their tall, narrow home had a steep staircase to each landing. They built into the wall of Corrie's upstairs bedroom a secret hiding place for the Jews in case there was ever a raid by the secret police. They conducted regular evacuation drills and lived perpetually on edge, never knowing when the Gestapo might arrive.

The dreaded raid came on February 28, 1944. It began suddenly, but quick-thinking Corrie was able to hide the Jews and members of the underground who were in the house behind the wall before the police could find them. All those in the hiding place later escaped.

The Gestapo took away the entire ten Boom family and locked them in prison. Corrie's father Casper, age 84, died ten days later. Corrie and her sister Betsie were eventually transferred to the infamous Ravensbruck concentration camp near Berlin, Germany, where Betsie died ten months later. A nephew, Kik, died from abuse and starvation in another camp.

Miraculously, Corrie was released from the concentration camp through a clerical error, and returned to Holland determined to help those who had suffered. After the war, she began receiving invitations from Christian groups in other countries asking her to speak about her experiences. At the end of one of her talks she was startled to see a man whom she recognized as one of the dreaded guards at Ravensbruck:

Corrie ten Boom's pure and simple message was the Gospel of Jesus Christ, with an emphasis on forgiving your enemies.

"One moment I saw the overcoat and the brown hat; the next, a blue uniform and a visored cap with its skull and crossbones. It came back with a rush: the huge room with its harsh overhead lights; the pathetic pile of dresses and shoes in the center of the floor; the shame of walking naked past this man. . . .

"The place was Ravensbruck and the man who was making his way forward had been a guard—one of the most cruel guards.

"Now he was in front of me, hand thrust out: 'A fine message, Fräulein! How good it is to know that, as you say, all our sins are at the bottom of the sea!'

"And I, who had spoken so glibly of forgiveness, fumbled in my pocketbook rather than take that hand. He would not remember me, of course—how could he remember one prisoner among those thousands of women?

"I was face-to-face with one of my captors and my blood seemed to freeze."

"But I remembered him and the leather crop swinging from his belt. I was face-to-face with one of my captors and my blood seemed to freeze.

" 'You mentioned Ravensbruck in your

talk,' he was saying. 'I was a guard there.' No, he did not remember me.

" 'But since that time,' he went on, 'I have become a Christian. I know that God has forgiven me for the cruel things I did there, but I would like to hear it from your lips as well. Fräulein,'—again the hand came out—'will you forgive me?'

"And I stood there—I, whose sins had again and again been forgiven—and could not forgive. Betsie had died in that place—could he erase her slow, terrible death simply for the asking?

"It could not have been many seconds that he stood there—hand held out—but to me it seemed hours as I wrestled with the most difficult thing I had ever had to do.

"For I had to do it—I knew that. The message that God forgives has a prior condition: that we forgive those who have injured us. 'If you do not forgive men their trespasses,' Jesus says, 'neither will your Father in heaven forgive your trespasses.'

"I knew it not only as a commandment of God, but as a daily experience. Since the end of the war I had had a home in Holland for victims of Nazi brutality. Those who were able to forgive their enemies were able also to return to the outside world and rebuild their lives, no matter what the physical scars. Those who nursed their bitterness remained invalids. It was as simple and as horrible as that. . . .

"Those [victims of Nazi brutality] who were able to forgive their enemies were able also to return to the outside world and rebuild their lives, no matter what the physical scars."

"And so woodenly, mechanically, I thrust my hand into the one stretched out to me. And as I did, an incredible thing took place. The current started in my shoulder, raced down my arm, sprang into our joined hands. And then this healing warmth seemed to flood my whole being, bringing tears to my eyes.

" 'I forgive you, brother!' I cried. 'With all my heart.'

"For a long moment we grasped each other's hands, the former guard and the former prisoner. I had never known God's love so intensely as I did then." [1]

REAL LIFE HELPS

The Bible says, "Bear with each other and forgive whatever grievances you may have against one another. Forgive as the Lord forgave you. And over all these virtues put on love, which binds them all together in perfect unity" (Colossians

Forgiveness is a hard decision that requires great spiritual strength.

3:13-14). Corrie had to choose to move past her bitter memories one by one. Forgiveness is given one act at a time, one hurt at a time, one person at a time. It is the right decision for a lot of reasons, including the basic point that it helps us! Those who forgive:

- Benefit from better immune systems and lower blood pressure
- Have better mental health than people who do not forgive
- Have lower amounts of anger, anxiety, and depression
- Enjoy more satisfying and long-lasting relationships

God draws near in forgiveness. Each day in your prayer life, make the choice to be a person of grace. It will not happen by accident.

PRAYER: Lord, teach me to forgive. Give me the heart of Jesus. I want to be one who forgives.

3

Forgiveness Comes From God

When you need help to forgive, seek God's heart; lean on His power.

Some people wear a small cross as a reminder that they belong to Jesus, the crucified Savior, Who forgives and invites us to forgive others. The following is a story of a soldier who witnessed the crucifixion of Jesus without recognizing its eternal impact.

The Soldier's Story

His work that day started out in an ordinary way, but it turned out to be special, a day to be celebrated. He could not contain his joy, because that day he had won a new coat.

He stopped by the office to clock out for the day. "Check it out! I'm styling today. Get a load of this coat!" Then on the way home from work, he just had to stop by the tavern to show it to his buddies. "Check out this new coat I got today. Can you believe it? Look at the fabric. This is some coat!"

His enthusiasm bubbled over as he walked into his house. I mean, the wife was not going to believe this one . . . a new coat, and such a fine one at that. "Honey, check it out. What do you think? Not a seam in it."

"That is a fine coat. How'd you get it?"

"Well, it started like a regular day at work," he said. "Me and the fellows were out on the hill like we always are. I was minding my cross; Tony and Rob, they were minding theirs. I had a fellow up on mine who the crowd really hated for some reason. They yelled at him, spat at him, cussed, mocked, and poked him. Even stuck some vinegar on a sponge and stabbed it around his mouth. I mean, they could not stand this guy. So me and the boys decided to cast lots for his coat. Not a bad coat for an old Jew. We cast lots and I won. Can you believe it?"

WHY IT IS "GOOD" FRIDAY

For this man, for his wife, for you, and even for me, Jesus died on the cross, and as they cast lots for His garments, Jesus looked down and said, "Father, forgive them, for they know not what they do." [1] What a glimpse of God's heart! We call the day that He died "Good Friday." Why "good"? Whom are we kidding?

On Jesus' day of humiliation He was brought before Pilate, taken by the guards, flogged, given a crown of thorns, mocked, hit in the face, and forced to carry His own cross.

We met pure love, God's love, and we rejected it, even killed it on a cross. How does Jesus' death finish forgiveness and offer eternal life?

Nailed to the cross, Jesus had a sign placed over His head as the soldiers gambled for His clothes. His only drink was wine—more like vinegar—thrust in His face on a sponge. This happened to the Son of God and we call it "good"? Worse than humiliation was the physical agony, the excruciating pain. The word "excruciating" comes from the Latin *excruciare*, literally "from the cross."

First, a soldier would nail the body to the cross—hands and wrist, then feet. Several soldiers would raise the cross and drop it into a hole with a jolt that caused more pain than the nailing itself. The victim's joints dislocated and tore apart, and the slow, painful process of death began. Slowly his shoulders sank. From his half kneeling position he would try to push with his feet to become more upright, but the nails tore at his flesh. The body's physical collapse was inevitable. Slowly the victim found it more difficult to breathe. The heart was beating rapidly because the lungs were starved for oxygen. Terrible agony ensued.

The cross is the simple, full expression of God's immense love for us, His children. The title deed to heaven for all believers is now in force.

Jesus hung on the cross fully exposed, naked to the sun and the elements, without food or drink . . . nothing. He could die from heart failure, asphyxiation, starvation, dehydration, exposure or any number of other causes. It was a dark day. How could anyone describe it as grand, glorious, or "good"? Good Friday? It really makes more sense to me how Germans look at Good Friday; they call it *Kar Freitag*, or Grief Friday.

As Jesus took His last breath, He said one word, "*Tetelestai*." "It is finished." *Tetelestai* was a common word, a conversational word of the times. It meant "complete," "finished," "whole," and even possibly "perfect." When an artist completed a painting with one final stroke, one word said it all, *"Tetelestai!"* When a father sent his son on a business mission and told him not to return until his business was completed, it was *"Tetelestai!"*

Jesus took His last breath on earth and uttered that final word, "Tetelestai!" It is finished! He had completed his Father's mission. He had paid the last penny on the debt.

Jesus died for the world. The sign nailed

over his head was written in Latin, Greek, and Hebrew—the three languages of the Roman Empire, the common man, and the Jew.

"For God so loved the world, that He gave His only begotten Son, that whosoever believeth in Him should not perish, but have eternal life" (John 3:16 KJV).

People explain His death in many ways: God demanded justice. He had to sacrifice something for our sins. God made a deal with Satan—the death of His Son for the souls of people—and then God tricked Satan with the resurrection. Jesus' suffering and agony on the cross show us the evil and sinister side of human nature. Whichever theory you choose, know this: God's plan is perfect. For Jesus, it is

You are forgiven, but that also means that God desires, even expects, that you will forgive others.

Grief Friday; but for us, it is Good Friday. Our sins are forgiven. We are whole and complete. Our forgiveness is real. Grace is ours.

Jesus said, "Father, forgive them, for they do not know what they are doing" (Luke 23:34).

REAL LIFE HELPS

(Galatians 3:27; Romans 6:11; Ephesians 4:22-24)

A simple way to understand God's forgiveness is to remember when you were baptized. He washed away your sin, made you a part of His family, and invited you to bring your sins, regrets, and deepest hurts to Him. He still washes them away. Remember, you became His when you were baptized! You belong to Jesus.

PRAYER: *Lord, I belong to You. You are the Supreme Forgiver. Show me the Way in Jesus, and show me Your way of forgiveness.*

4

Forgiveness Helps Families

The pain is deepest when you're hurt by those closest to you.

Family forgiveness is one of the hardest kinds there is. It often requires you to take the first step, even when it is not welcomed or invited.

Jeanette's mother died as she was giving birth to her daughter, and a short time later Jeanette's father, Woodrow, and his five children moved in with his mother-in-law. Two years later, Woodrow abandoned his children, leaving them for his mother-in-law and his 16-year-old son Paul to raise.

From that time on, Woodrow's life became a downward alcoholic spiral. Once or twice a year he would drop in to see his children in the middle of the night when Paul was able to track him down. Paul became the only father Jeanette knew.

This was how Jeanette recalled her biological father's logic for his drive-by visits:

"We were on welfare, and the welfare agency would have gotten him for abandonment and made him pay child support, so he never came when anyone could see him. As a child I remember how he would bring a sock full of change and give it to me, tell me why he left, act as if everything was normal, and tell me that he had no choice but to leave us.

"The social workers would interview me when they came for home visits to make sure nothing had changed, and I was told I couldn't tell them I had seen my father. I didn't really understand this because my grandmother drilled into us to tell the truth always, but my brother was very protective of my father. Paul could remember that he had been a good father.

"My grandmother completely disapproved of my father and, in fact, told me that God would understand why she couldn't forgive him."

When Jeanette was very young her brother took her to Jacksonville to see her father, who was working at a store. She said, "I remember, because I got candy. My brother made sure my father knew he had no rights to me and that my brother was the only father I had known."

Jeanette said, "I began to think I needed to track my father down to let him know I forgave him for leaving us."

In college, Jeanette began to think about Jesus on the cross. As her faith grew, she considered "how God had forgiven us of all the bad things we did. I began to think I needed to track my father down to let him know I forgave him for leaving us." She called and told him, "It might not matter to you, but I want you to know I forgive you for leaving us." She said that he immediately began to justify himself because his mother-in-law had made it difficult for him to date or to do anything, and he couldn't take it. She recalled, "I simply said to him, 'I just wanted you to know I forgive you,' and said goodbye.

"It struck me how he continued to blame everyone else when he was the one who left his five children with an old woman on welfare and a 16-year-old boy. My brother worked at the

"It struck me how he continued to blame everyone else when he was the one who left his five children with an old woman on welfare and a 16-year-old boy."

farmers' market and at a chicken farm to help support us while he finished high school."

Even as Jeanette extended her hand in grace, her own father still could not—or would not—receive it. The forgiveness was all one-sided. Jeanette was freed from the power of her father's abandonment, but her father was not. In fact, her father never stepped out of his own failure to move toward redemption and restoration. He never escaped the consequences and tragedy of his own actions, even when his daughter offered the chance. Grace extended, and grace rejected.

Forgiveness is not condoning. It is not being a doormat for others to walk on. It is an offer of strength.

Jeanette's offer of mercy released her spirit, but that does not mean that she did not hold her father accountable. Forgiveness does not erase consequences, but it offers a new start.

When Jeanette's father began to age and needed help, her brother once again stepped in and bought a small trailer, put it on his own land and let their father live there. However, one weekend while the family was out of town, Woodrow was drinking and he took his son's farm truck and wrecked it. Jeanette drove home from college and told her father that her brother had cleaned up his messes repeatedly and that she would not allow that any more.

"Be kind and compassionate to one another, forgiving each other, just as in Christ, God forgave you"
(Ephesians 4:32).

REAL LIFE HELPS

Behavior has consequences. Forgiveness does not erase them, but it has the power to bring release. Forgiveness has the power to release you from the bondage of past hurts and insults and move forward. Jeanette forgave her father and moved into God's future. She did not look back with unforgiveness but focused on the future with gratitude, giving thanks for a brother and his wife and a grandmother who cared for her and loved her when her own father did not.

Unforgiveness is a dead end. Forgiveness gives you a future.

Pray that you can be a peacemaker in your relationships by using this 13th century prayer of St. Francis of Assisi as a regular part of your prayer life. Ask God to change your heart rather than the heart of someone else. Watch God work in your life as you become an instrument of God's peace.

PRAYER. *Lord, make me an instrument of your peace;*
Where there is hatred, let me sow love;
Where there is injury, pardon;
Where there is doubt, faith;
Where there is despair, hope;
Where there is darkness, light;
And where there is sadness, joy.

O Divine Master,
Grant that I may not so much seek
To be consoled, as to console;
To be understood, as to understand;
To be loved, as to love;
For it is in giving, that we receive,
It is in pardoning, that we are pardoned;
And it is in dying, that we are born to eternal life. [3]

5

Forgiveness Is A Journey

Forgiveness is a process that takes resolve, patience, and prayer.

In the spring of 1995 Julie Marie Welch was a bright, 23-year-old young woman with a promising future. Just 5′1″ and 103 pounds, she packed a lot of zest into a small package. After graduating from Marquette University as a foreign language major, Julie had returned to her hometown of Oklahoma City to work for the

Social Security Administration as a translator for clients who struggled with English. She had recently discovered anew the power of faith in her life and had even met Eric, her soon-to-be fiancé, at a young singles' prayer meeting.

On Wednesday morning, April 23, 1995, Julie attended Mass, as was her custom, and then went to her office on the first floor of the Murrah Federal Building. Early in the day, she walked out to the waiting area to receive a client and as she was in the corridor on her way back to her office, Timothy McVeigh detonated a bomb that killed her and 167 other people. McVeigh would later claim that his violent act was his revenge on the federal government for what he saw as oppressive and abusive actions against the Branch Davidian cult in Waco, Texas. McVeigh chose that day, the second anniversary of the inferno that had consumed David Koresh and his followers in Waco, for the Murrah Building bombing.

At the time of the explosion, Julie's father, Bud, turned on the television to see a three-story pile of rubble where the Murrah Building had been. Right then, he lost hope for his daughter's survival. Ironically, no one in Julie's work area was hurt. If she had returned seconds earlier, she would have survived.

I first met Julie's father by phone, and then in person. His deep eyes communicated clearly how much he had loved his daughter. For days after the blast, full of pain and anger, he drove to the site to remember, to reflect, and to wonder where to go from here. The first months of grief were the worst experience of his life. He wanted vengeance on McVeigh—a quick and violent execution. Nothing more, nothing less.

Bud began to self-medicate with alcohol each night from the moment he returned home from work at his Texaco station until he passed out. His hangovers grew increasingly worse, and his cigarette habit shot from one to four packs per day. Slowly but surely, Bud Welch was destroying himself. The pain was too great.

Finally, in January 1996, Bud drove to the bomb site again. As he stood across the street, his head still aching from the night before, he thought to himself, "I have to do something different, because what I am doing now is not working." Vengeance had been McVeigh's motivation, and he could see where that had led—an ugly bomb site, a daughter gone forever, and the soul of a father riddled with anguish. He began to change from wanting McVeigh to be executed to simply wanting him to be tried and convicted. Wanting the death penalty felt too much like revenge. He began his first steps toward healing by speaking against the death penalty at colleges and universities. By June 1998 he was well on his

Bud didn't know the answer, but he knew it was not revenge.

way to overcoming his addiction to alcohol and cigarettes and was exploring what to do next.

About this time, Bud received an invitation to meet with Bill McVeigh, Tim's father. A Catholic nun had arranged the visit for a time when Bud was to speak in the Buffalo, New York, area. With great anxiety, Bud walked up to the house where Tim had spent much of his life. The ghosts haunting Bud were almost too much for him, but he went ahead with the meeting with Bill, whom he had seen only on television shortly after the bombing.

Even in that painful time right after Julie's death, Bud had been able to see in Bill McVeigh's eyes the pain of a father whose son had gone terribly astray.

Bud and Bill walked and talked in the garden for 30 minutes and then went into the house where Tim's sister, Jennifer, joined them at the table. Their conversation unfolded slowly and nervously, but Bud knew he was in the right place. He could not help but notice a large 8x10 photo of Tim McVeigh hanging on the wall. Feeling that Bill and Jennifer were probably self-conscious about how often he was looking at the photo, Bud suddenly blurted out, "My, what a good looking kid."

Bill replied, "Bud, can you cry?"

Bud said, "Yes, why?"

Bill had confided earlier that he had not cried for years, but at that moment, a large tear rolled down his cheek. As Bud stood to leave, the three of them—Bud, Bill, and Jennifer—embraced. Bud and Bill shook hands, then Bud hugged Jennifer once more and they began to sob. Later, Bud recalled that he sobbed more than he ever had before or since as an adult. He could see the love of a father in the eyes of Bill McVeigh.

Bud's journey of forgiveness took five long years after Julie's tragic death. He still cannot explain how the process takes place, only that it takes time, patience, and prayer. When Bud sees pain etched on the faces of those Oklahoma City victims' families who have been unable to forgive, he knows from his own experience that anger leads to resentment, which leads to bitterness and spiritual death. Occasionally, a flash of anger and regret returns when Bud sees a young woman who reminds him of Julie, or when he dreams that he has seen Julie alive again, but then he moves forward, knowing that to live in the past is to die.[4] When Tim was executed in 2001, Bud, who already knew the pain of a father having to bury a child, now shared that pain with Bill McVeigh.

Often forgiveness does not come in a moment, but takes time for the healing to be complete.

Real Life Helps

At the end of this book is a forgiveness journal where you can list the names of people whom you have hurt and need to ask for their forgiveness. On the next journal page you can list people who have hurt you whom you need to forgive. A forgiveness journal continues the process of forgiveness instead of allowing old hurts or hang-ups to build up inside. You will grow in grace and holiness by forgiving.

"Now instead, you ought to forgive and comfort him, so that he will not be overwhelmed by excessive sorrow"
(2 Corinthians 2:7)

PRAYER. *Help me to be willing to take the journey toward forgiveness. Even if it takes time for the healing to be complete, I want to be a person who forgives.*

6

Forgiveness Offers A New Future

When you're been wronged, you can focus on the past or God's future.

You have probably never heard of Thomas Doswell, because he spent 19 of the best years of his life in prison for a rape he did not commit. Doswell, a black man, was convicted of the 1986 rape of a 48-year-old white woman at a hospital in Pittsburgh. He was sentenced to 13 to

26 years in prison. At the time, he was 25 years old and the father of two young children.

During nearly two decades in prison, he was denied parole four times because he claimed he was innocent and consistently refused to acknowledge responsibility for the rape. In 2005 his innocence was proven when a judge finally ordered that evidence obtained from the victim be tested for DNA. Prosecutors opposed it, but the Innocence Project of the Benjamin N. Cardozo School of Law at Yeshiva University[5] assisted Doswell and his attorney in demanding that the testing be done. The results proved that the semen taken from the victim was not his. A week later prosecutors agreed to join Doswell's motion to vacate his conviction and sentence and he was released.

The victim and another witness had identified Doswell from a group of photos shown to them by police. At the time, Pittsburgh police marked mug shots of people charged with rape with the letter "R." Doswell had insisted that the witnesses identified him as the rapist only because an "R" appeared under his picture. Since that time, police no longer mark photos as "R."

Most people in his situation would have been angry and resentful, but instead while he was in prison he had earned a degree, learned to speak Spanish, and mastered seven instruments including guitar, saxophone, flute, drums, and trumpet. "Having the faith I have in Jesus has taught me that I couldn't walk around for 20 years with anger bottled up in me," said Doswell. "It would have killed me. It would have done more damage to me than good." [6]

Nineteen years is a long time to build resentment toward prosecutors, accusers, police officers, and the legal system that has imprisoned you, but Doswell belongs to Jesus.

Upon his release from prison his mother, Olivia, led a crowd of tearful, smiling relatives and friends in chanting, "God is good."

Doswell forgave the police officer, whom he believed had focused on him because he had been acquitted of sexual assault a year earlier. He forgave the rape victim, who had identified him despite clear differences between his appearance and that of the assailant. He forgave the prosecutors who fought his appeals and who tried to stop DNA testing.

"Help us, O God our Savior, for the glory of your name; deliver us and forgive our sins for your name's sake" (Psalm 79:9).

While in prison Doswell's sons grow up. He missed his father's funeral, weeping as he listened in on the telephone while singing "Amazing Grace." He said, "Despite being away from your family and being away from your freedom that you had always rightfully deserved to have, God has blessed me and I managed to come through it in a positive light."[7] He said he can get on with the rest of his life because he knows the power of forgiveness.

REAL LIFE HELPS

Being kind to someone who has taken advantage of you prevents you from feeling resentful, and can also change *their* heart.

Watchman Nee told the story of a Chinese Christian who owned a rice paddy next to one owned by a Communist. He irrigated his paddy by pumping water out of a canal using a leg-operated pump that looks like a bicycle. Every day, after the Christian had pumped enough water to fill his field, the Communist would come out, remove some boards that kept the water in the Christian's field, and let all the water flow down into his own field. That way, he didn't have to pump any water for himself. This injustice continued day after day until finally the Christian prayed, "Lord, if this keeps up, I'm going to lose all my rice, maybe even my field. I've got a family to care for. What can I do?"

The Lord answered. The next morning the Christian arose in the predawn hours and pumped water into the field of his Communist neighbor. Then he replaced the boards and pumped water into his own rice paddy. In a few weeks both fields of rice were doing well—and the Communist became a Christian.

Showing kindness prevents resentment and anger from accumulating in your soul.

PRAYER. *Good God, replace the resentment in my heart with kindness. Give me a heart like yours.*

7

FORGIVENESS GIVES OFFENDERS GRACE

God's grace is revealed to sinners when believers show forgiveness.

To most people, giving grace to those who deserve vengeance seems unjust, but grace is a breathtaking snapshot of the heart of God. In forgiving, you experience the radical nature of God's love and grace, and you feel God's heart.

The following story of the triumph of forgiveness over vengeance is told by Philip

Yancey in his book *Rumors of Another World.* [8]

"Nelson Mandela taught the world a lesson in grace when, after emerging from prison after twenty-seven years and being elected president of South Africa, he asked his jailer to join him on the inauguration platform. He then appointed Archbishop Desmond Tutu to head an official government panel with a daunting name, the Truth and Reconciliation Commission. Mandela sought to defuse the natural pattern of revenge that he had seen in so many countries where one oppressed race or tribe took control from another.

"Do not repay anyone evil for evil. Be careful to do what is right in the eyes of everybody. If it is possible, as far as it depends on you, live at peace with everyone" (Romans 12:17-18).

"For the next two-and-a-half years, South Africans listened to reports of atrocities coming out of the TRC hearings. The rules were simple: if a white policeman or army officer voluntarily faced his accusers, confessed his crime, and fully acknowledged his guilt, he could not be tried and punished for that crime. Hard-liners grumbled about the obvious injustice of letting criminals go free, but Mandela insisted that the country needed healing even more than it needed justice.

When you forgive, you break the cycle of bitterness and anger. Instead of endlessly striking out at those who hurt you, causing them to strike back, you forgive, and you have peace.

"At one hearing, a policeman named van de Broek recounted an incident when he and other officers shot an eighteen-year-old boy and burned the body, turning it on the fire like a piece of barbecue meat in order to destroy the evidence. Eight years later van de Broek returned to the same house and seized the boy's father. The wife was forced to watch as policemen bound her husband on a woodpile, poured gasoline over his body, and ignited it.

"Do not take revenge, my friends, but leave room for God's wrath, for it is written: 'It is mine to avenge; I will repay,' says the Lord"
(Romans 12:19).

"The courtroom grew hushed as the elderly woman who had lost first her son and then her husband was given a chance to respond.

" 'What do you want from Mr. van de Broek?" the judge asked. She said she wanted van de Broek to go to the place where they burned her husband's body and gather up the dust so she could give him a decent burial. His head down, the policeman nodded agreement.

"Then she added a further request, 'Mr.

van de Broek took all my family away from me, and I still have a lot of love to give. Twice a month, I would like for him to come to the ghetto and spend a day with me so I can be a mother to him. And I would like Mr. van de Broek to know that he is forgiven by God, and that I forgive him too. I would like to embrace him so he can know my forgiveness is real.'

"Spontaneously, some in the courtroom began singing 'Amazing Grace' as the elderly woman made her way to the witness stand, but van de Broek did not hear the hymn. He had fainted, overwhelmed."

" If your enemy is hungry, feed him; if he is thirsty, give him something to drink. In doing this, you will heap burning coals on his head.' Do not be overcome by evil, but overcome evil with good"

(Romans 12:20-21).

REAL LIFE HELPS

Visualize your deepest hurts and resentments as a bag of rocks. Each rock represents a hurt—a time when you were stung by someone's unkind words or harmful actions.

In your imagination, place that bag of rocks in the trunk of your car, drive to a nearby lake, and throw them in. All the hurts, grudges and resentments that you were carrying are now in the bottom of the lake. You no longer carry them in your mind. You have left them there, permanently. They are gone. The cycle is broken.

PRAYER: *Lord, help me to release the grudges and resentments that I carry deep within. May Your grace touch my heart and the heart of those who have hurt me.*

8

Forgiveness Breaks The Death Cycle

Forgiveness ends the cycle of revenge that leads to spiritual death.

I still remember vividly how as an eight-year-old boy I discovered the joy of the 1972 Olympics. All the pageantry and fanfare of the nations of the world were in one place, for one purpose—to compete. I loved sports, and these were the greatest. I was glued to the television, but I had no idea what was to come.

At 4:30 AM on September 5, some American athletes who had been out partying were sneaking into the Olympic Village. Unknown to them, the eight men in tracksuits sneaking in with them were carrying duffel bags loaded with guns and grenades. They were members of the Palestinian terror group Black September on a mission to kidnap the Israeli Olympic team.

Once inside, the terrorists used stolen keys to enter two apartments being used by the Israeli team at 31 Connollystrasse, Buildings 1 and 3. Israeli fencing champion Dani Alon was asleep in a second-floor room of Building 2 when he was awakened by a loud bang. "What's that?" asked his roommate, fencer Yehuda Weisenstein.

"Probably some other team celebrating," Alon said. "Go back to sleep." Minutes later, three of his teammates—two shooters and a wrestler—burst into the room, terrified. Sheer chaos! Alon ran to the window, trying to make sense where there was none.

Outside, a man in a white hat was talking to two policemen. "We have killed two already," the man in the white hat was saying. "We have nine more inside. Get the Israeli government on the phone or we kill everybody." Lying on the ground bleeding was the wrestling coach, Moshe Weinberg.

I still remember vividly as a boy watching that Olympic terrorist on television. He became the symbol of Black September.

Sneaking a look through the balcony door, Alon could see another man who was wearing a ski mask and carrying a machine gun. I still remember vividly as a boy watching that terrorist on television. He became the symbol of Black September. Alon and his teammates talked furtively about how the team shooters could use their competition guns to fire bullets into the head of the man in the white hat, then run for it. But they wondered what that would accomplish besides alerting the terrorists to the fact that they had missed a building.

The athletes decided to sneak down the stairs to the living room, slip out the sliding glass doors, and run. Alon recalled later, "As I jumped the fence, I was looking at the man in the mask, and he was looking at me. For some reason, he didn't shoot. He never shot."

While the world watched the man in the ski mask on TV, the terrorists continued their threats and negotiations, then took the Israeli hostages to the military airport in Munich for a flight to the Middle East. That flight never took off. Within hours, the nine remaining Israeli hostages and many of the terrorists were dead, killed at the airport in a botched rescue attempt.

After that tragedy in Munich, Alon never returned to fencing, and until recently he didn't want to talk about what happened. He was troubled by nightmares and outbursts of anger. Then in 2006, 10,000 people heard Dani Alon, the old fencer, now 61, speak about his experience. It was the opening ceremony of the Maccabi Games held in Phoenix for Jewish athletes. Many stayed afterward to shake his hand.

"You are forgiving and good, O Lord, abounding in love to all who call on you" *(Psalm 86:5).*

One of the Black September attackers is still alive today. When a reporter asked Alon what he would do if he met him face to face, his response to the vicious attack may surprise you. "I'd forgive him," Alon said. "He was so young. He was a soldier. I have been a soldier too. We have to make peace. All this bloodshed only leads to more bloodshed." [9]

Forgiveness breaks the death cycle.

REAL LIFE HELPS

Where the sad cycle of unforgiveness reigns, vengeance and more violence result. The Middle East experiences this cycle nearly every day. Killing triggers more killing. Cease-fires end. Violence continues. Forgiveness is absent. The cycle never seems to end. Only forgiveness, with God's supernatural power, can break the cycle. Make forgiveness a centerpiece of your prayer life each day. It may change you more than it changes others. That is good.

PRAYER: *Lord, only You have the power to break the cycle of unforgiveness and revenge. The cycle continues in my heart and in the world. I need Your help. I cannot do it on my own power, but You are forgiving and good. May Your love abound in my life and in the world around me.*

9

Forgiveness Heals Emotional Wounds

When bitterness and hatred are gone,

emotional wounds can heal.

On September 15, 1979, twenty-two-month-old Joel Sonnenberg was riding in a car with his father and uncle heading for a vacation in Maine. Behind them in another car were Joel's mother, his aunt, and his three-year-old sister. They were all in line at the Hampton Toll Booth in New Hampshire when a 36-ton tractor trailer truck slammed into the line of cars. The green Chevy where little Joel was riding burst into flames. Joel's father and uncle escaped with their clothing and hair on fire, each thinking the other had Joel. A 20-year-old motorist named Michael Saraceni heard Joel's cries and heroically pulled him out, saving his life.

The toddler was a mass of ashes. His arms were charred. His hair was gone.

Joel was a mass of ashes. His arms were charred. His hair was gone. His face was black and his body smoldering. He was rushed to a nearby hospital and then to Harvard Medical Complex. He was given just a ten percent chance of survival. Next he was moved to the Shriners' Burn Institute where he stayed for four and a half months and had countless surgeries.

Miraculously, Joel survived, but he grew up with a disfigured face, and scar tissue covered most of his body. He experienced how cruel the world can be when stares and comments followed him everywhere. People left restaurants because his face disturbed them. He could never escape the evidence of the tragic accident.

In the midst of his distress, he was able to grow in the Holy Spirit and gain remarkable patience—not only with God but also with other people.

When Joel was in high school, his family moved to the small western North Carolina community of Montreat, where Joel captained his high school soccer team, and became an Eagle Scout. He met Jesus personally at Montreat Presbyterian Church. Later he went on to college and graduated from Taylor University, and has since written an inspiring autobiography, *Joel*, published by Zondervan. For the 1996 Olympics, he bravely carried the flame through his community in his one remaining hand.

Eventually he endured more than 45 surgeries, suffering inexpressible physical pain and the emotional distress of stares and harmful words like "Take off your mask." In spite of all that, Joel says, "The greatest times in my life are when I reflect and see what God has done—all the provisions He has had for me. I say, 'Wow' there's got to be a higher hand in this. Jesus is the answer.

"As I've gotten older," Joel said, "I have been shown by the Lord that it's a true gift to be different. That's my purpose: to show that God is good."

"As I've gotten older, I have been shown by the Lord that it's a true gift to be different. That's my purpose: to show that God is good. He loves others just as much as He loves me." [10] His patience is other-worldly, even divine. Joel understands grace.

In 1998, Joel's patience came into plain view. Reginald Dort, the truck driver who rammed into the stopped cars at the toll booth, had jumped bail and fled to Canada after the accident and continued driving a truck. He avoided the law until 1997 when he was arrested during a routine safety check. He was then sent to New Hampshire for sentencing.

The Sonnenberg family spoke at Dort's sentencing for second degree assault. Joel was the last family member to address the court. He looked in the eyes of the man who had caused his years of anguish and said, "This is my prayer for you . . . that you may know that our Lord and Savior Jesus Christ's grace has no limits." [11]

Commenting on Joel's autobiography, *Publisher's Weekly* said, "However tragic his story, Sonnenberg's recounting of his young life resounds in hope as he takes every opportunity to speak about how God has given him the courage to succeed." [12]

Forgiveness and grace differentiate Christians from the followers of every other religion. No other faith possesses these traits at its very heart. The Koran, for example, rarely mentions forgiveness. It never describes God as "love." Not once. Grace does not lie at the center of Islam as it does in Christianity. Christians can practice their faith and share it with the world through forgiveness.

"For as high as the heavens are above the earth, so great is His love for those who fear Him; as far as the east is from the west, so far has He removed our transgressions from us" *(Psalm 103.11-12).*

REAL LIFE HELPS

If you would like to do something positive about this message of forgiveness, write a letter to someone who has hurt you very much. You may choose to mail it later or you may not, but writing the letter is an important step toward your healing and the release of the other person from your unforgiveness. In your letter, express the hurt you have experienced. Write it out in detail. Share with the person how you feel. Then express that you forgive the person who has hurt you so deeply.

God forgives.
God forgives instantly.
God forgives freely.
God forgives completely.

Feel the burden being lifted as you offer forgiveness. It doesn't matter whether or not the person is willing to receive your forgiveness or even acknowledge that what they did was wrong.

This letter gives you the chance to say things exactly as you wish to say them. Be a person of grace. Extend forgiveness even as you describe your pain. You may at some point choose to mail the letter if the person is still living or you know where they are. Again, their response is not the important factor. Your offer of forgiveness is the key. The letter unleashes the power of forgiveness in your life.

Our sins are not unforgivable. All of us stand before God in need of grace. Our problems are different to be sure—but we are all the same—sinners.

PRAYER: *Lord, pour out your healing grace on my heart. I want to release others from the pain I carry. I desire your freedom and release. Come, Lord Jesus.*

10

Forgiveness Never Gives Up

When you are like God,

you never give up on sinners.

In this final chapter, I want to share a dramatic story that imagines what might have happened when Jesus gave a sinner a second chance. It is told from the perspective of someone who was watching the God of forgiveness in action.

The Scribe's Story

I have always loved to read and study, so when my father told me that I had been chosen to be a scribe, it just seemed to fit. Studying, reading, copying scrolls and books—that was me, a Jewish scribe. Perfect!

I enjoyed scribe school more than most of my friends. Knowing the fine points of the Law played to my strengths. Hebrew became my passion; the Scriptures, my first love. God's Law is perfect, and I got to share that perfection with the Jews around me. I loved the fact that people came to me to discover God's will and His words. As scribes, we enjoyed power and respect. Prestige came with the position, and I liked that. I settled marriage disputes, navigated business deals gone bad, and

"As scribes, we enjoyed power and respect. Prestige came with the position, and I liked that."

resolved arguments between neighbors. I interpreted the Law and determined who was right and wrong. I was a scribe, a man of God.

The day I met Jesus started out not much different from any other. Some men had found one of their married friends in bed with a woman. Adultery! The evidence was obvious. I mean, she was practically naked before us. As a scribe, I knew that the sin of adultery was one of God's Top Ten. The Scriptures were clear. The woman's fate was decided; death by stoning was the only answer. In fact, the only question was whether the man should also be punished by death. We had our rocks and we were ready.

"If any one of you is without sin, let him be the first to throw a stone at her" (John 8:7-8).

But Solomon, one of the Pharisees, wanted to make a point. We were tired of this

Jesus fellow and all the hoopla everywhere He went. His teaching seemed to dazzle everybody. Didn't folks know that we scribes were the ones who *really* knew the Scriptures? After all, God put us in charge, didn't He?

Solomon persuaded us to drag the woman in front of Jesus when He was teaching in front of the temple. Folks were enthralled. We saw our chance. This time, we would expose Jesus as a fraud and an impostor. We placed the adulterous woman right in front of Him and reminded Him, "In the law Moses commanded us to stone such a woman. Now what do you say?" We knew we could catch Jesus this time and bring Him to justice.

". . . for all have sinned and fall short of the glory of God, and are justified freely by his grace through the redemption that came by Christ Jesus"

(Romans 3:23-24).

Then it happened. I mean, it was weird. There we were, a crowd of people, a half-naked woman, some scribes and Pharisees, and Jesus. We asked Him a question, and He bent over and started writing with his finger on the ground. What is that? So Solomon kept questioning him. "You know what the Law says. What do you say about that? You have heard what Moses said. What about you?" Still Jesus stayed bent over. We peppered Him with questions, and He said nothing. We just knew we had Him, and then He said something. He straightened up and said to us, "Let anyone among you who is without sin be the first to throw a stone at her."

" 'Then neither do I condemn you,' Jesus declared. 'Go now, and leave your life of sin' " (John 8:11).

Of course, we had sins. We had no idea what to do, so one-by-one, we dropped our rocks, and walked away. Later I heard that Jesus asked the woman, "Woman, where are they? Is there no one left to condemn you?"

She said, "No sir."

Then Jesus said something I still cannot figure out. He looked her in the eye and said, "Then neither do I condemn you. Go your way, and do not sin again." Who was He to contradict Moses? Jesus forgave her sin. Right then, right there. What do you do with that?

REAL LIFE HELPS

Accept God's forgiveness once and for all in your life. Make His forgiveness your own.

PRAYER: *God, I want to believe that You forgive me. Way down deep in my soul, I want to know. Pour out Your forgiveness. Lavish Your grace upon me right now, that I may be changed, that I may be wholly and completely Yours.*

CONCLUDING WORD

Jesus is all about forgiveness.

Remember this about Jesus. He gets on this forgiveness thing, and He won't let it go. Everywhere Jesus goes, He either teaches about forgiveness or He extends it to someone. Every place you open the Gospels, Jesus is sounding the bugle about forgiveness. Jesus, very simply, is all about forgiveness. That teaches us how very important forgiveness is to our God. That is why I have written this little book.

When Jesus preaches for the first time in the Gospel of Matthew, what is the first word out of His mouth? *Repent!* At the top of His lungs, *Repent!* "Turn around, you are going in the wrong direction!" *Repent!* In other words, you need forgiveness.

Jesus taught His disciples to pray, *"Forgive us our trespasses, as we forgive those who trespass against us."* Right in the middle of praying, Jesus sounds the trumpet of forgiveness.

To make matters worse, when Jesus finishes the Lord's Prayer, He immediately feels the need to expand even more on forgiveness:

"For if you forgive men when they sin against you,
your heavenly Father will also forgive you.
But if you do not forgive men their sins,
your Father will not forgive your sins"
(Matthew 6:14-15).

What is the only part of the Lord's Prayer Jesus feels compelled to explain further? The part about forgiveness.

Me? I would have preferred that He had expanded a bit on "Lead us not into temptation but deliver us from the evil one" (Matthew 6:13). That's where I want some clarification. But Jesus takes the opportunity to sound His bugle one more time about forgiveness.

Jesus makes it plain. We need forgiveness. He's not making a suggestion here. He is stating the truth, sounding a bugle, and He won't let it go. You and I need forgiveness, forgiveness from God and from one another. You may already know that. Scripture says that every one of us falls short of the glory of God (Romans 3.23) and that not one of us is righteous (Ecclesiastes 7:20). We need forgiveness. We fail to do the will of God. We regularly choose the lower path instead of the higher. We try to satisfy ourselves with something other than God. We allow things to take first

"There is not a righteous man on earth who does what is right and never sins" (Ecclesiastes 7:20).

place in our hearts and come before Him. We try to please ourselves rather than Him. We use words to inflict wounds.

In fact, Jesus' whole mission is forgiveness. God's plan for the whole world is forgiveness and reconciliation. That is God's work, forgiveness. That is God's heart. We have turned our backs on Him, and He desires to make us right. Our hearts have wandered. So He sends Jesus to tell us to repent, to point the way home, to show God's love, and finally to die on the cross doing what we cannot do for ourselves, take away our sin. When you look at the cross, you see the very heart of God.

Jesus—the Son of God
Led out to die alongside two criminals
Comes to the place called the Skull
where they crucify Him.
Men below cast lots for His clothes
People stand watching;
rulers sneering; soldiers mocking.
"Are you the Christ? Save yourself and us!"
And on the cross, Jesus, Lamb of God,
looks down on them and says,

"Father, forgive them,
for they do not know what they are doing"
(Luke 23:34).

We need forgiveness and God wants to forgive. He yearns to forgive. His very heart is forgiveness, but Jesus does not stop there.

Look again at forgiveness: *Forgive us our trespasses as we forgive those who trespass against us.*

Look at that phrase closely, "*as we forgive those who trespass against us.*" Notice these words again as He explains the Lord's Prayer, as He expands on forgiveness in case we didn't get it the first time. Jesus is not just saying that we need forgiveness. In fact, Jesus takes it one step further. He makes a direct tie, a conditional link: if you are not able to forgive others, God will not forgive you. God binds Himself to the promise that as you forgive others, He will forgive you.

> *"Do not be deceived: God cannot be mocked. A man reaps what he sows. The one who sows to please his sinful nature, from that nature will reap destruction; the one who sows to please the Spirit, from the Spirit will reap eternal life"*
> *(Galatians 6:7-8).*

If you are not in a state of forgiveness with other people, you cannot be in a forgiven relationship with God. That is a hard truth. If we do not forgive others, there is no forgiveness for us. Again, don't listen to me; listen to Jesus.

> Peter: "*How many times shall I forgive my brother when he sins against me? Seven?*"
>
> Jesus: "*Not seven but seventy times seven.*"
>
> *(See Matthew 18:21-22.)*

Jesus just won't let this forgiveness thing go. This is important to Him. Listen to Him. Forgiveness is important. Jesus is clear:

1. We need forgiveness.
2. There is no forgiveness without forgiveness; we must give in order to receive.

That is the basic law of the harvest and of the Kingdom of God (Galatians 6:7-8). Do you want love? Then give love. Do you want to receive peace? Give peace. Do you want forgiveness? Give it. The more you learn to forgive, the more forgiveness you will receive. The more you live a lifestyle of forgiveness, the less you will be affected by bitterness, grudges, and resentment.

When you clench your fists, fold your arms, and grit your teeth—in anger or hatred toward someone—you leave no room in your heart for God to forgive you. There simply is no room for God to place His hand in yours.

The lesson is simple. Give forgiveness and unleash a flood of grace from heaven, lavishing God's grace on people around you and on yourself.

Many blessings on you for a
life rooted in forgiveness—
the deep expression of the love of God.

END NOTES

1. "I'm Still Learning to Forgive" by Corrie ten Boom is reprinted with permission from *Guideposts* magazine. Copyright 1972 by Guideposts, Carmel, New York 10512. All rights reserved.
2. Thanks to Fred Craddock and his interpretations of the Gospel accounts.
3. Francis of Assisi, "The Prayer of Saint Francis" (*United Methodist Hymnal* # 481).
4. From personal conversations with Bud Welch.
5. Information on the Thomas Doswell case online at The Innocence Project of the Benjamin N. Cardozo School of Law at Yeshiva University http://innocenceproject.org/case/display_profile.php?id=163.
6. Bill Moushey, "Man goes free after 19 years in prison for rape he did not commit. DNA testing exonerates Thomas Doswell, who speaks of forgiveness" (*Pittsburgh Post-Gazette*, August 02, 2005). Online at http://www.post-gazette.com/pg/05214/547399.stm.
7. Ibid.
8. Excerpted from *Rumors of Another World* by Philip Yancey, copyright © 2003. This excerpt is by permission of Zondervan, www.zondervan.com.

All rights reserved. Read the rest of this book when you purchase it from your favorite retailer. This excerpt may be copied and forwarded only if this permission paragraph is retained intact.

9. Rick Reilly, "A Survivor's Tale" (*Sports Illustrated*, 7/31/2006). Available online at http://www.jewishtoronto.com/content_display.html?ArticleID=191282.
10. Randy Bishop, "Not the Man in the Mirror" (*Today's Christian*, November/December, 1998, Vol. 36, No.6, p. 65). Online at http://www.christianitytoday.com/tc/8r6/8r6065.html. See also Joel Sonnenberg's website at http://www.joel.cc/pages/home.asp.
11. Bishop, "Not the Man in the Mirror."
12. *Publisher's Weekly*. Copyright © Reed Business Information, a division of Reed Elsevier Inc. All rights reserved.

FORGIVENESS JOURNAL

People whom you have hurt and need to ask their forgiveness

Forgiveness Journal

People who have hurt you whom you need to forgive